REVIEW COPY
COURTESY OF
CAPSTONE PRESS

Great Inventions

THE SEWING MACHINE

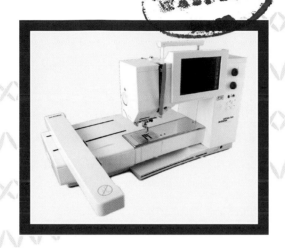

by Rebekah Dorn

Consultant:
Shelly Burge
American Representative
International Sewing Machine Collector's Society
Lincoln, Nebraska

Capstone
press

Mankato, Minnesota

Fact Finders is published by Capstone Press
151 Good Counsel Drive, P.O. Box 669, Mankato, Minnesota 56002
www.capstonepress.com

Library of Congress Cataloging-in-Publication Data
Dorn, Rebekah.
    The sewing machine / by Rebekah Dorn.
    p. cm.—(Fact finders. Great inventions)
    Includes bibliographical references and index.
    ISBN 0-7368-2670-X (hardcover)
    1. Sewing machines—Juvenile literature. [1. Sewing machines. 2. Inventions.] I. Title.
II. Series.
TJ1510.D67 2005
681'.7677—dc22   2003027663

Summary: Introduces the history and development of the sewing machine and explains
    how a sewing machine works.

Editorial Credits
Christopher Harbo, editor; Juliette Peters, series designer; Patrick Dentinger, book designer
    and illustrator; Kelly Garvin, photo researcher; Eric Kudalis, product planning editor

Photo Credits
Capstone Press/Gary Sundermeyer, 1, 21, 22, 27 (all)
Comstock Inc., cover
Corbis/Bettmann, 5, 13, 26 (left); Brownie Harris, 24–25
Getty Images/Hulton Archive, 14, 15, 26 (middle, right)
Mary Evans Picture Library, 11
Singer Sewing Company, 16–17, 18, 19
Stock Montage Inc., 6–7

1 2 3 4 5 6 09 08 07 06 05 04

Table of Contents

Chapter 1

Howe's Idea

In 1837, Elias Howe moved to Boston. He worked in a shop fixing and building machines. One day, Howe heard his boss talking to a customer. The customer said that anyone who invented a working sewing machine could make a great deal of money.

For eight years, Howe worked on making a sewing machine. In 1845, he showed his machine to the public. Howe hoped to get rich by selling many machines, but no one placed an order.

Howe did not give up. He worked on improving his sewing machine. On September 10, 1846, Howe received a U.S. **patent** on his second machine.

Elias Howe's sewing machine was powered by a hand-cranked wheel.

Chapter 2

Before the Sewing Machine

Before sewing machines, people sewed everything by hand. They used needles and thread to make blankets, clothes, and curtains. Sewing by hand was hard work. It was hard on the eyes and it hurt the hands. Sewing clothes for a family took a long time. Many people only owned one or two outfits.

Early Needles

People have been hand sewing for more than 20,000 years. Early needles were made out of wood or animal bone. By the 1300s, needles were made out of iron.

▲ Before sewing machines, people had to sew everything made with cloth by hand.

In the 1400s, the first iron eyed needles were made. An eyed needle has a small loop, or eye, to hold thread. These needles could pass through cloth easily and make tight stitches.

Chapter 3

Early Sewing Machines

By the late 1700s, several people had ideas for sewing machines. These inventors worked in different countries. They may not have always known what other inventors were building.

Early Designs and Models

In 1790, Thomas Saint of England received a patent for his sewing machine idea. Saint planned a machine cranked by hand. His machine would have a single thread and a straight needle. The hand crank would drive the needle and thread through leather. His machine would sew leather shoes and boots. No one knows if he ever built his machine.

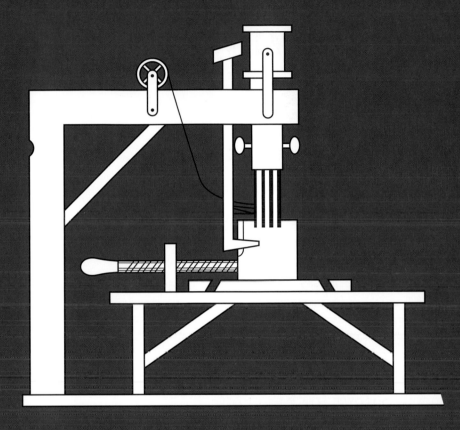

▲ Thomas Saint's idea was a sewing machine that pushed a single thread and needle through leather. This drawing is based on a sketch of his machine from the Smithsonian Institution in Washington, D.C.

In 1804, Thomas Stone and James Henderson received a French patent for a sewing machine. It sewed curved and straight **seams**. Their machine used a motion similar to hand sewing. It was used to join the edges of cloth together.

In 1807, Edward Walter Chapman received a British patent for a sewing machine. His machine used two needles. It could make belts and cloth bands.

In 1830, Barthelemy Thimmonier from France invented a sewing machine. He was the first person to use a sewing machine in a business. His factory had 80 sewing machines. The workers sewed uniforms for the French army.

FACT!

Tailors near Thimmonier's factory were afraid sewing machines would take away their jobs. They broke into Thimmonier's factory and smashed his machines.

Barthelemy Thimmonier (bottom) invented a sewing machine (top) to use in his business. His machine was an important step between hand sewing and machine sewing.

11

Walter Hunt

In the early 1800s, people began making sewing machines in the United States. In 1834, Walter Hunt invented the first **lockstitch** sewing machine. As a needle and thread passed through cloth, the thread made a loop. A second thread passed through the loop and locked the stitch in place.

Elias Howe

In 1846, Elias Howe received a U.S. patent for a sewing machine. The machine used a metal plate with pins to hold cloth. The plate and pins pulled the cloth forward as a needle sewed. The needle moved from side to side. Howe's machine stitched a few inches (centimeters). Then, the cloth was reloaded on the pins.

In the 1860s, Elias Howe used posters like this one to help sell his sewing machines.

▲ Isaac Singer's first sewing machine was powered with a hand crank.

Isaac Singer

In 1851, Isaac Singer received a patent for a sewing machine. His machine sewed long seams. Its needle moved up and down. Later, Singer invented a foot pedal called a **treadle**. Pumping the treadle turned gears. These gears moved the needle up and down.

Legal Problems

Legal problems soon grew between Howe and Singer. Singer said he got ideas from Hunt's sewing machine. But Howe believed Singer had taken ideas from his own machine instead.

Howe took Singer to court for the rights to his invention. Howe believed he should share any money Singer made on his sewing machines. In 1854, Howe won the court battle. Singer had to pay Howe some money for each machine sold. Both Singer and Howe became millionaires.

A woman sews with a 1902 Singer sewing machine. It was ▼ powered by a treadle.

15

Chapter 4

Better Sewing Machines

By the late 1800s, more than 200 U.S. companies made sewing machines. Clothing factories used many of the first sewing machines. In 1856, the Singer Manufacturing Company built sewing machines for the home.

Electric Sewing Machines

By 1935, most sewing machines ran on electricity. Electric machines helped make sewing faster. In the home, people mended and made clothes quickly. In factories, more clothes were made in less time. Clothing prices began to drop. People could now own more than one or two outfits.

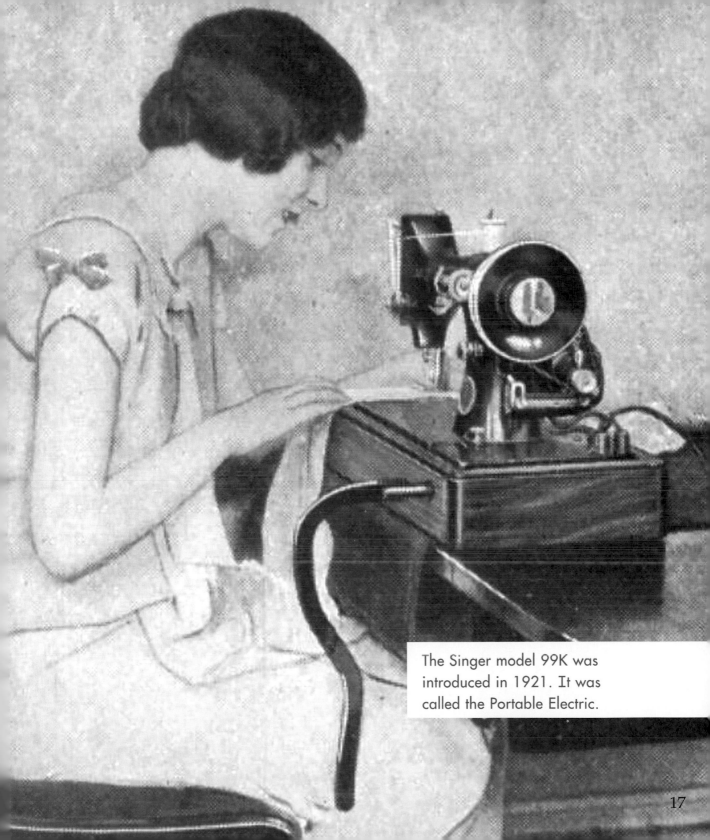

The Singer model 99K was introduced in 1921. It was called the Portable Electric.

Zigzag Machines

By the 1930s, some machines were made to sew zigzag stitches. These stitches made wide jagged lines instead of thin straight lines. Zigzag stitches made the seams in clothing stronger.

F A C T !

In 1873, Helen Blanchard of Portland, Maine, received a patent for the first zigzag sewing machine.

The Singer Slant-O-Matic went on sale in 1952. It sewed zigzag stitches.

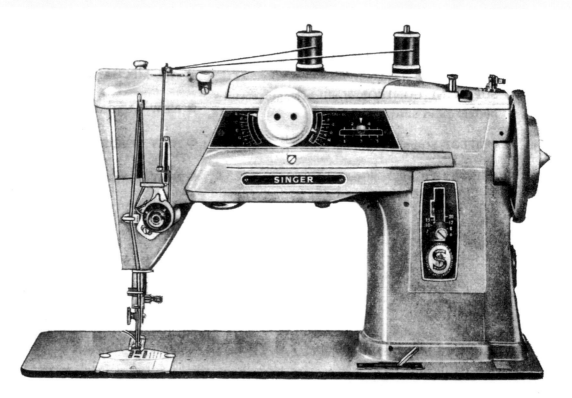

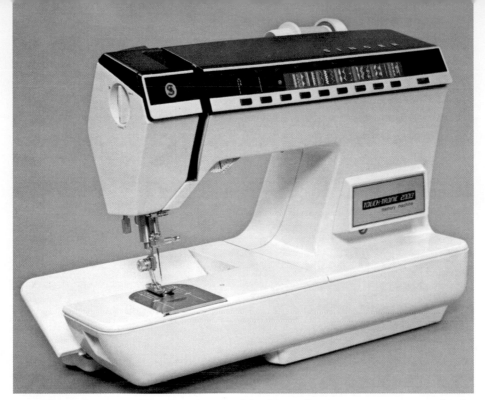
▲ The Athena 2000 was the world's first electronic sewing machine.

Electronic Machines

In 1975, the Singer Company built
the first electronic sewing machine
for the home. The Athena 2000 used
a built-in computer. The computer
controlled the motor's speed and
needle position. Electronic machines
gave people more control over the
stitches they sewed.

Chapter 5

How Sewing Machines Work

A sewing machine uses a needle with an eye just above the sharp point. The thread from the spool goes through the needle's eye. The needle is fastened to a needle bar. The bar is driven up and down by a motor. A person runs the motor by pressing a foot pedal.

When the motor starts, the bar pushes the needle and thread through the cloth. The cloth is held by a **presser foot**. A **feed dog** is underneath the presser foot. Ridges on the feed dog pull the cloth along while the needle goes up and down.

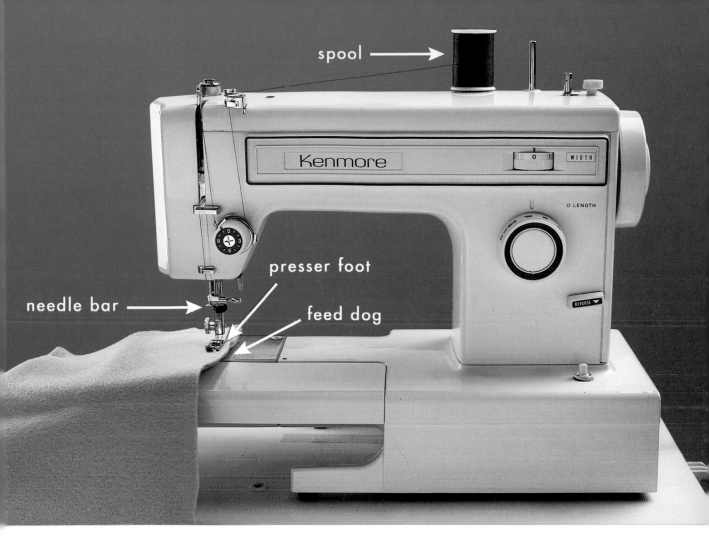

spool

Kenmore

0 LENGTH

WIDTH

REVERSE ▼

presser foot

needle bar

feed dog

⬆ A sewing machine's presser foot holds the cloth as the needle moves up and down.

FACT!

The feed dog on a sewing machine has nothing to do with pets or dog food. In machinery, the word "dog" means something that holds or bites. The word "feed" means movement of the material. The metal teeth of the feed dog hold and move the material as the machine sews it.

The Lockstitch

Sewing machines still use a lockstitch to join cloth. Sewing machines make the lockstitch with the bobbin and shuttle hook. The bobbin is a spool of thread that sits below the feed dog. It sits inside the shuttle hook. The shuttle hook spins as the needle rises and falls through the cloth.

A bobbin case holds the bobbin in place. The bobbin and the case sit inside the shuttle hook.

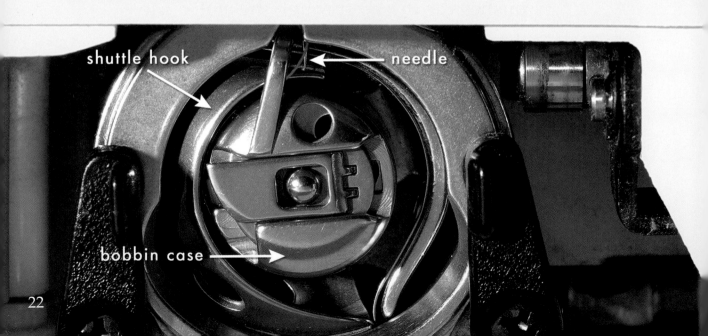

shuttle hook

needle

bobbin case

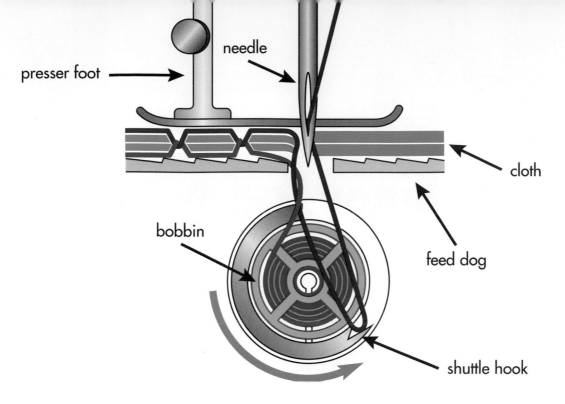

presser foot

needle

cloth

bobbin

feed dog

shuttle hook

▲ A lockstitch forms when the top and bottom threads wrap together.

To make the lockstitch, the needle pushes the thread through the cloth. The thread forms a loop that is caught by the shuttle hook. The shuttle hook then pulls the loop around the bobbin thread. As the needle pulls up, the two threads tighten and lock. The wrapped threads make the stitch strong.

Chapter 6

Sewing Machines Today

Sewing machines and their uses have changed since the 1800s. Machines today are faster. Many machines can make more than one type of stitch. Some machines are built to do only one special job. Clothing factories use sewing machines that sew just pockets or just button holes.

Factories use sewing machines to make products besides clothing. Tents, backpacks, sails, and flags are all made with sewing machines. Factory workers use sewing machines to make blankets and curtains. Sewing machines even sew together the cloth that covers furniture.

▲ Factory workers make clothing and other cloth products quickly with the help of sewing machines.

The use of sewing machines in the home has also changed. Some people still use sewing machines to make their own clothes. But the sewing machine is also an important tool for crafts and hobbies.

Embroidery

Embroidery is one craft people can do with their sewing machines. Embroidery is stitching that uses thread to make pictures and words.

The Bernina artista 200 is one of the newest embroidery sewing machines. It can be connected to a home computer to download images. The sewing machine then sews the images on cloth.

Sewing Machines through the Years

Singer's Sewing Machine

1851

Howe's Sewing Machine

1846

Singer Treadle Sewing Machine

1940

Lasting Importance

Sewing machines have changed people's lives. Factories use machines to make clothes and other products faster and for less cost. People buy towels and sheets instead of making them. Sewing machines also make life easier at home. People spend less time mending or making clothes. They also use sewing machines for fun crafts and hobbies.

Singer Slant-O-Matic
1961

Kenmore Model 1212
1974

Bernina artista 200
2002

Fast Facts

- In 1790, Thomas Saint became the first person to patent his ideas for a sewing machine.

- In 1830, Barthelemy Thimmonier became the first person to use sewing machines in a business.

- Walter Hunt invented the first lockstitch sewing machine in 1834.

- On September 10, 1846, Elias Howe received a U.S. patent for a sewing machine.

- A foot pedal called a treadle, invented by Isaac Singer, made sewing easier in the 1850s.

- Most sewing machines ran on electricity by 1935.

- In 1975, the Singer Company built the Athena 2000. It was the first electronic sewing machine for home use.

Hands On: Machine Advantage

Before the sewing machine, people had to sew clothes by hand. Try this activity to compare hand sewing and machine sewing. Ask an adult to help you use the sewing machine.

What You Need

scissors
white thread
measuring tape

sewing needle
4 scraps of dark-colored cloth
sewing machine

What You Do

1. Cut a piece of thread about 12 inches (30 centimeters) long.
2. Thread the needle and pull the thread through so it is doubled. Tie the ends of the thread together.
3. Place two pieces of cloth on top of each other.
4. Begin sewing the cloth together along one edge. Push the needle through both pieces of cloth. Then push it back through the other way.
5. Continue pushing the needle in and out. Sew in a straight line until you reach the end of the cloth. Tie a knot so the thread doesn't come out.
6. Ask an adult to help you set up the sewing machine.
7. Place the other two pieces of cloth together. Use the sewing machine to sew a straight line along one edge of the cloth. When you are done, cut the thread and tie a knot at each end.
8. Compare your hand sewing with the machine sewing. Which sewing method made a stronger stitch? Which way was quicker?

Glossary

embroidery (em-BROI-duh-ree)—a form of sewing used to sew pictures or words on cloth

feed dog (FEED DAWG)—a ridged piece of metal on a sewing machine that moves cloth along under the needle

lockstitch (LOK-stich)—a stitch formed when one thread passes through cloth and wraps around another thread

patent (PAT-uhnt)—a document that protects people's inventions so others cannot steal the ideas

presser foot (PRESS-ur FUT)—a metal piece that holds cloth against the feed dog of a sewing machine

seam (SEEM)—a line of sewing that joins two pieces of cloth

treadle (TREH-duhl)—a lever pumped by a person's foot to drive a machine

Internet Sites

FactHound offers a safe, fun way to find Internet sites related to this book. All of the sites on FactHound have been researched by our staff.

Here's how:
1. Visit *www.facthound.com*
2. Type in this special code **073682670X** for age-appropriate sites. Or enter a search word related to this book for a more general search.
3. Click on the **Fetch It** button.

FactHound will fetch the best sites for you!

Read More

Carlson, Laurie M. *Queen of Inventions: How the Sewing Machine Changed the World.* Brookfield, Conn.: Millbrook Press, 2003.

Parker, Steve. *Textiles.* Science Files. Materials. Milwaukee: Gareth Stevens, 2002.

Index